It's Our Anniversary!

ANNIVERSARY YEAR _____

CELEBRATING _____ YEARS

·················· *How we Celebrated* ··················

_____
_____
_____
_____
_____
_____
_____
_____
_____
_____
_____

·················· *What Our Year Was Like* ··················

_____
_____
_____
_____
_____
_____
_____
_____
_____
_____
_____

Highlights

Challenges

Plans & Goals for the Next Year

PHOTO

It's Our Anniversary!

ANNIVERSARY YEAR _____

CELEBRATING _____ YEARS

·················· *How we Celebrated* ··················

_____

_____

_____

_____

_____

_____

_____

_____

_____

·················· *What Our Year Was Like* ··················

_____

_____

_____

_____

_____

_____

_____

_____

_____

Highlights

Challenges

Plans & Goals for the Next Year

· · · · · · · · · · · · · · · · · · · ·

PHOTO

It's Our Anniversary!

ANNIVERSARY YEAR _____

CELEBRATING _____ YEARS

·················· *How we Celebrated* ··················

_____
_____
_____
_____
_____
_____
_____
_____
_____
_____

·················· *What Our Year Was Like* ··················

_____
_____
_____
_____
_____
_____
_____
_____
_____
_____

Highlights

Challenges

Plans & Goals for the Next Year

PHOTO

It's Our Anniversary!

ANNIVERSARY YEAR _____

CELEBRATING _____ YEARS

.... *How we Celebrated* ....

_____
_____
_____
_____
_____
_____
_____
_____
_____
_____

.... *What Our Year Was Like* ....

_____
_____
_____
_____
_____
_____
_____
_____
_____
_____

Highlights

Challenges

Plans & Goals for the Next Year

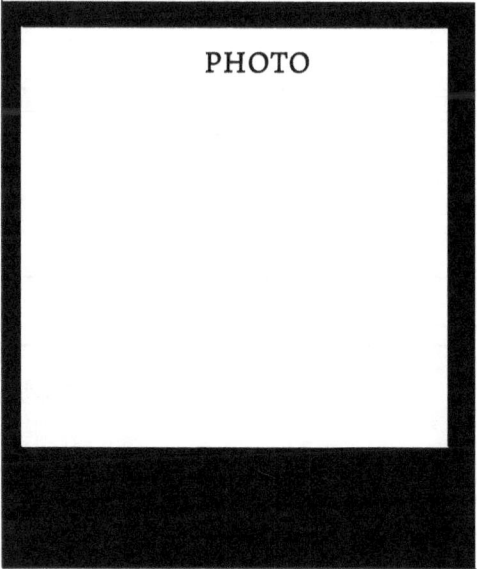

PHOTO

It's Our Anniversary!

ANNIVERSARY YEAR _____

CELEBRATING _____ YEARS

················· How we Celebrated ·················

_____
_____
_____
_____
_____
_____
_____
_____
_____

················· What Our Year Was Like ·················

_____
_____
_____
_____
_____
_____
_____
_____
_____

Highlights

Challenges

Plans & Goals for the Next Year

PHOTO

It's Our Anniversary!

ANNIVERSARY YEAR _____

CELEBRATING _____ YEARS

·················· *How we Celebrated* ··················

_____
_____
_____
_____
_____
_____
_____
_____
_____
_____

·············· *What Our Year Was Like* ··············

_____
_____
_____
_____
_____
_____
_____
_____
_____
_____

Highlights

Challenges

Plans & Goals for the Next Year

_____
_____
_____
_____
_____
_____
_____

• •

_____
_____
_____
_____
_____
_____
_____

PHOTO

It's Our Anniversary!

ANNIVERSARY YEAR _____

CELEBRATING _____ YEARS

·················· How we Celebrated ··················

_____

_____

_____

_____

_____

_____

_____

_____

·················· What Our Year Was Like ··················

_____

_____

_____

_____

_____

_____

_____

_____

Highlights

Challenges

Plans & Goals for the Next Year

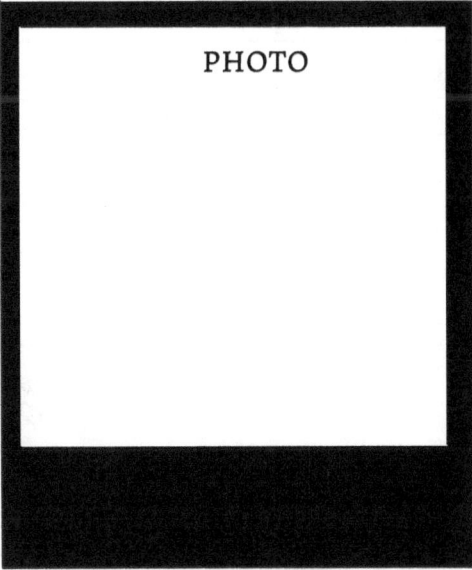

PHOTO

It's Our Anniversary!

ANNIVERSARY YEAR _____

CELEBRATING _____ YEARS

······················ *How we Celebrated* ·····················

_____
_____
_____
_____
_____
_____
_____
_____
_____

················· *What Our Year Was Like* ·················

_____
_____
_____
_____
_____
_____
_____
_____
_____
_____

Highlights

Challenges

Plans & Goals for the Next Year

· ·

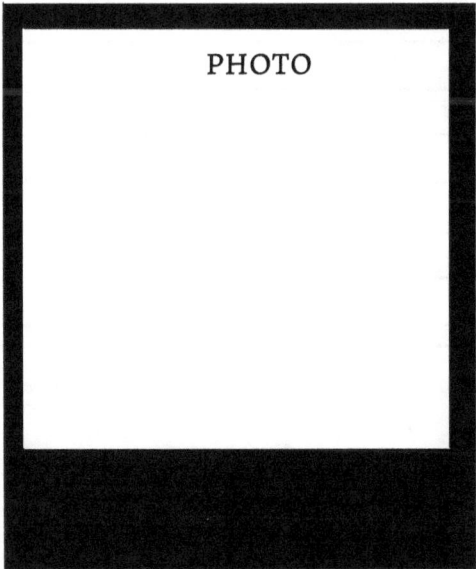

PHOTO

It's Our Anniversary!

ANNIVERSARY YEAR _____

CELEBRATING _____ YEARS

····················· *How we Celebrated* ·····················

_____

_____

_____

_____

_____

_____

_____

_____

_____

·················· *What Our Year Was Like* ··················

_____

_____

_____

_____

_____

_____

_____

_____

Highlights

Challenges

Plans & Goals for the Next Year

_____
_____
_____
_____
_____
_____

• • • • • • • • • • • • • • • • • • • •

_____

_____

_____

_____

_____

_____

_____

PHOTO

It's Our Anniversary!

ANNIVERSARY YEAR _____

CELEBRATING _____ YEARS

·················· *How we Celebrated* ··················

_____
_____
_____
_____
_____
_____
_____
_____
_____

·················· *What Our Year Was Like* ··················

_____
_____
_____
_____
_____
_____
_____
_____
_____

Highlights

Challenges

Plans & Goals for the Next Year

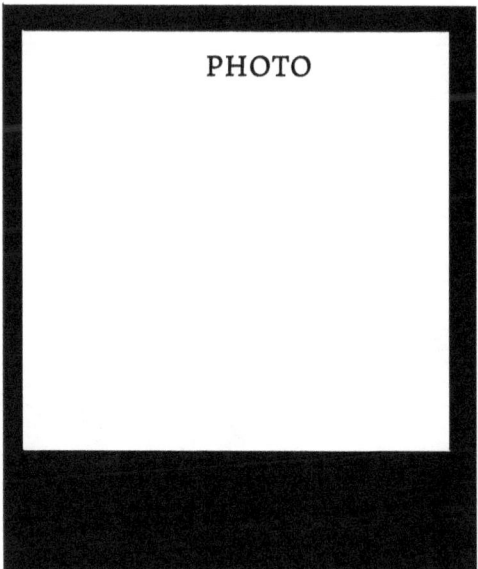

PHOTO

It's Our Anniversary!

ANNIVERSARY YEAR _____

CELEBRATING _____ YEARS

.... *How we Celebrated* ....

_____
_____
_____
_____
_____
_____
_____
_____
_____
_____

.... *What Our Year Was Like* ....

_____
_____
_____
_____
_____
_____
_____
_____
_____

Highlights

Challenges

Plans & Goals for the Next Year

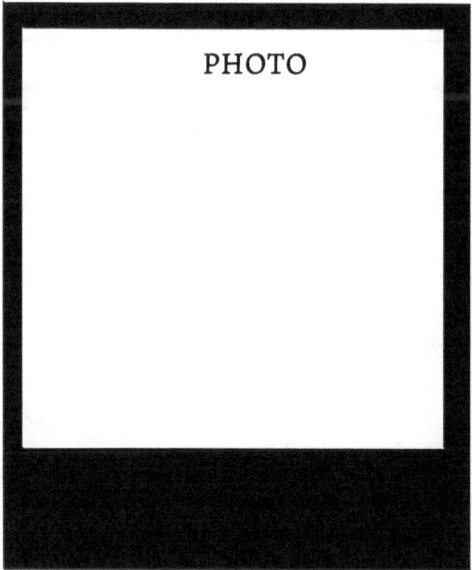

PHOTO

It's Our Anniversary!

ANNIVERSARY YEAR _____

CELEBRATING _____ YEARS

················· *How we Celebrated* ·················

_____
_____
_____
_____
_____
_____
_____
_____

················· *What Our Year Was Like* ·················

_____
_____
_____
_____
_____
_____
_____
_____

Highlights

Challenges

Plans & Goals for the Next Year

_____

_____

_____

_____

_____

_____

_____

• • • • • • • • • • • • • • • • • • • •

PHOTO

It's Our Anniversary!

ANNIVERSARY YEAR _____

CELEBRATING _____ YEARS

·················· *How we Celebrated* ··················

_____

_____

_____

_____

_____

_____

_____

_____

_____

·················· *What Our Year Was Like* ··················

_____

_____

_____

_____

_____

_____

_____

_____

Highlights

Challenges

Plans & Goals for the Next Year

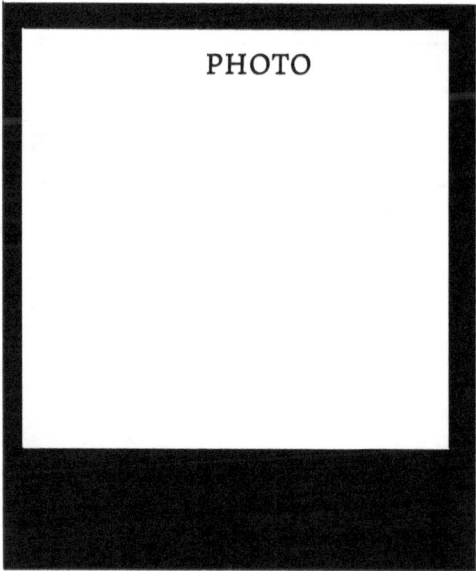

PHOTO

It's Our Anniversary!

ANNIVERSARY YEAR _____

CELEBRATING _____ YEARS

·················· How we Celebrated ··················

_____
_____
_____
_____
_____
_____
_____
_____
_____
_____

·················· What Our Year Was Like ··················

_____
_____
_____
_____
_____
_____
_____
_____
_____

Highlights

Challenges

Plans & Goals for the Next Year

PHOTO

It's Our Anniversary!

ANNIVERSARY YEAR _____

CELEBRATING _____ YEARS

·············· *How we Celebrated* ···············

_____
_____
_____
_____
_____
_____
_____
_____
_____
_____

················ *What Our Year Was Like* ················

_____
_____
_____
_____
_____
_____
_____
_____
_____

Highlights

Challenges

Plans & Goals for the Next Year

PHOTO

It's Our Anniversary!

ANNIVERSARY YEAR _____

CELEBRATING _____ YEARS

·················· *How we Celebrated* ··················

_____
_____
_____
_____
_____
_____
_____
_____
_____

·················· *What Our Year Was Like* ··················

_____
_____
_____
_____
_____
_____
_____
_____

Highlights

Challenges

Plans & Goals for the Next Year

_____
_____
_____
_____
_____
_____

• • • • • • • • • • • • • • • • • • • •

_____

_____

_____

_____

_____

_____

_____

PHOTO

It's Our Anniversary!

ANNIVERSARY YEAR _____

CELEBRATING _____ YEARS

·················· How we Celebrated ··················

_____
_____
_____
_____
_____
_____
_____
_____

·················· What Our Year Was Like ··················

_____
_____
_____
_____
_____
_____
_____
_____

Highlights

Challenges

Plans & Goals for the Next Year

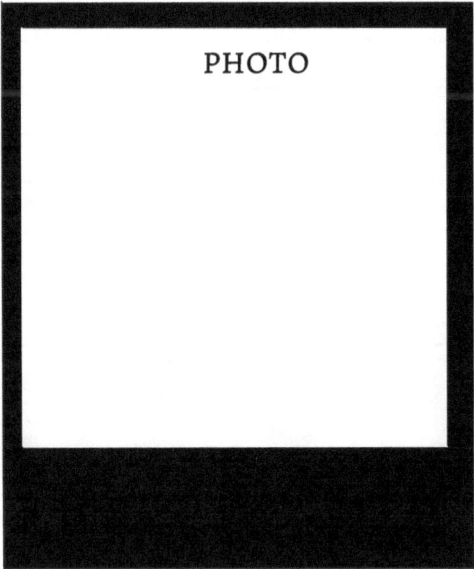

PHOTO

It's Our Anniversary!

ANNIVERSARY YEAR _____

CELEBRATING _____ YEARS

·················· *How we Celebrated* ··················

_____

_____

_____

_____

_____

_____

_____

_____

·················· *What Our Year Was Like* ··················

_____

_____

_____

_____

_____

_____

_____

_____

Highlights

Challenges

Plans & Goals for the Next Year

PHOTO

It's Our Anniversary!

ANNIVERSARY YEAR _____

CELEBRATING _____ YEARS

·················· How we Celebrated ··················

_____
_____
_____
_____
_____
_____
_____
_____
_____

·················· What Our Year Was Like ··················

_____
_____
_____
_____
_____
_____
_____
_____

Highlights

Challenges

Plans & Goals for the Next Year

PHOTO

It's Our Anniversary!

ANNIVERSARY YEAR _____

CELEBRATING _____ YEARS

·················· *How we Celebrated* ··················

_____
_____
_____
_____
_____
_____
_____
_____

··············· *What Our Year Was Like* ···············

_____
_____
_____
_____
_____
_____
_____
_____

Highlights

Challenges

Plans & Goals for the Next Year

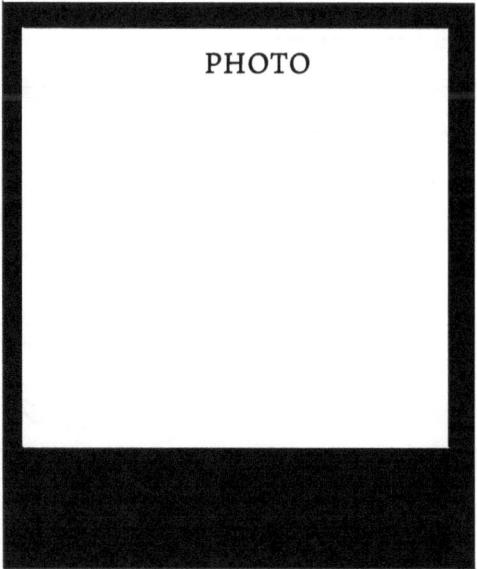

PHOTO

It's Our Anniversary!

ANNIVERSARY YEAR _____

CELEBRATING _____ YEARS

···················· *How we Celebrated* ····················

_____
_____
_____
_____
_____
_____
_____
_____

···················· *What Our Year Was Like* ····················

_____
_____
_____
_____
_____
_____
_____
_____

Highlights

Challenges

Plans & Goals for the Next Year

PHOTO

It's Our Anniversary!

ANNIVERSARY YEAR _____

CELEBRATING _____ YEARS

·················· How we Celebrated ··················

_____
_____
_____
_____
_____
_____
_____
_____
_____
_____

·················· What Our Year Was Like ··················

_____
_____
_____
_____
_____
_____
_____
_____
_____

Highlights

Challenges

Plans & Goals for the Next Year

PHOTO

It's Our Anniversary!

ANNIVERSARY YEAR _____

CELEBRATING _____ YEARS

·············· *How we Celebrated* ··············

_____
_____
_____
_____
_____
_____
_____
_____

·············· *What Our Year Was Like* ··············

_____
_____
_____
_____
_____
_____
_____
_____

Highlights

Challenges

Plans & Goals for the Next Year

PHOTO

It's Our Anniversary!

ANNIVERSARY YEAR _____

CELEBRATING _____ YEARS

················· *How we Celebrated* ·················

_____
_____
_____
_____
_____
_____
_____
_____
_____

················· *What Our Year Was Like* ·················

_____
_____
_____
_____
_____
_____
_____
_____
_____

Highlights

Challenges

Plans & Goals for the Next Year

PHOTO

It's Our Anniversary!

ANNIVERSARY YEAR _____

CELEBRATING _____ YEARS

·················· *How we Celebrated* ··················

_____
_____
_____
_____
_____
_____
_____
_____
_____

·················· *What Our Year Was Like* ··················

_____
_____
_____
_____
_____
_____
_____
_____
_____
_____

Highlights

Challenges

Plans & Goals for the Next Year

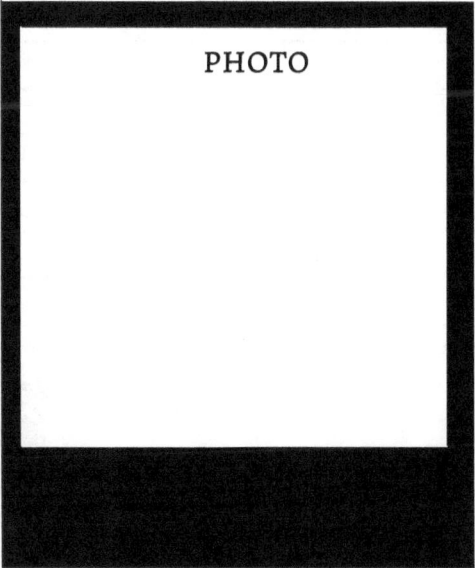

PHOTO

It's Our Anniversary!

ANNIVERSARY YEAR _____

CELEBRATING _____ YEARS

·················· How we Celebrated ··················

_____
_____
_____
_____
_____
_____
_____
_____

·················· What Our Year Was Like ··················

_____
_____
_____
_____
_____
_____
_____
_____

Highlights

Challenges

Plans & Goals for the Next Year

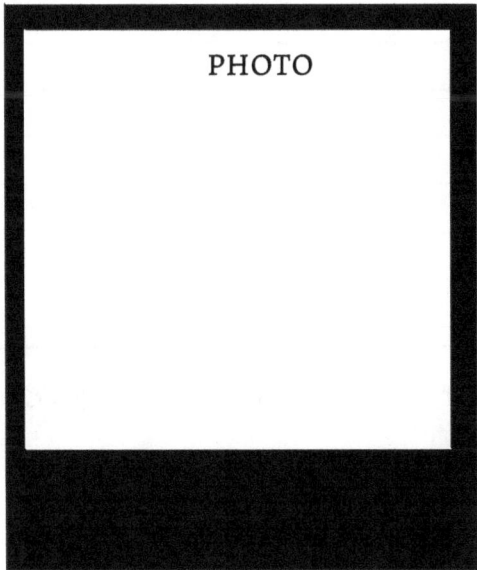

PHOTO

It's Our Anniversary!

ANNIVERSARY YEAR _____

CELEBRATING _____ YEARS

·················· *How we Celebrated* ··················

_____
_____
_____
_____
_____
_____
_____
_____
_____
_____

··············· *What Our Year Was Like* ···············

_____
_____
_____
_____
_____
_____
_____
_____
_____
_____

Highlights

Challenges

Plans & Goals for the Next Year

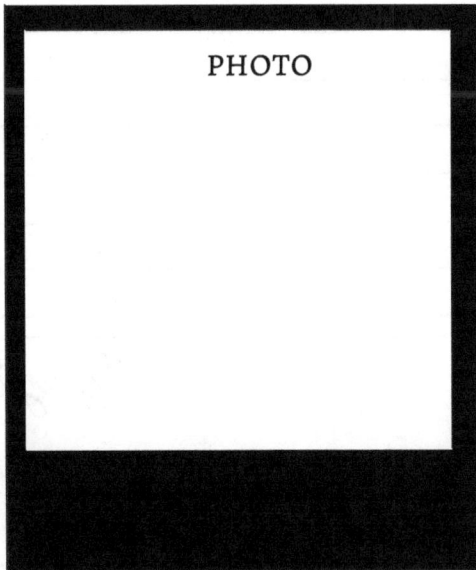

PHOTO

It's Our Anniversary!

ANNIVERSARY YEAR _____

CELEBRATING _____ YEARS

·················· *How we Celebrated* ··················

_____
_____
_____
_____
_____
_____
_____
_____
_____

·················· *What Our Year Was Like* ··················

_____
_____
_____
_____
_____
_____
_____
_____
_____
_____

Highlights

Challenges

Plans & Goals for the Next Year

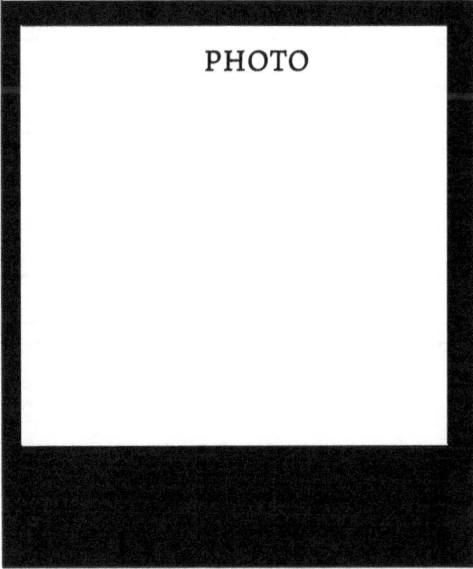

PHOTO

It's Our Anniversary!

ANNIVERSARY YEAR _____

CELEBRATING _____ YEARS

···················· *How we Celebrated* ····················

_____
_____
_____
_____
_____
_____
_____
_____
_____

···················· *What Our Year Was Like* ····················

_____
_____
_____
_____
_____
_____
_____
_____

Highlights

Challenges

Plans & Goals for the Next Year

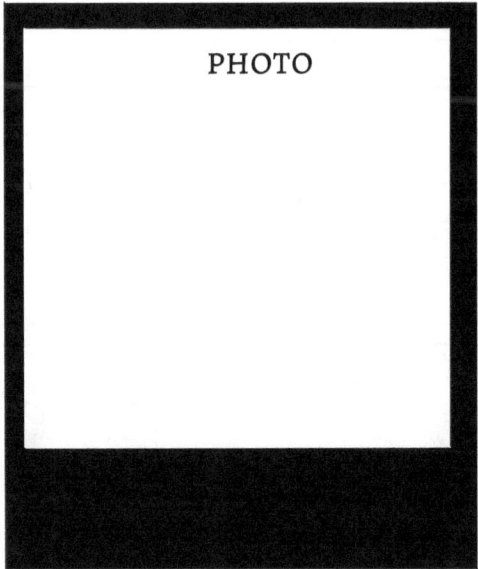

PHOTO

It's Our Anniversary!

ANNIVERSARY YEAR _____

CELEBRATING _____ YEARS

···················· *How we Celebrated* ····················

_____
_____
_____
_____
_____
_____
_____
_____
_____

···················· *What Our Year Was Like* ····················

_____
_____
_____
_____
_____
_____
_____
_____

Highlights

Challenges

Plans & Goals for the Next Year

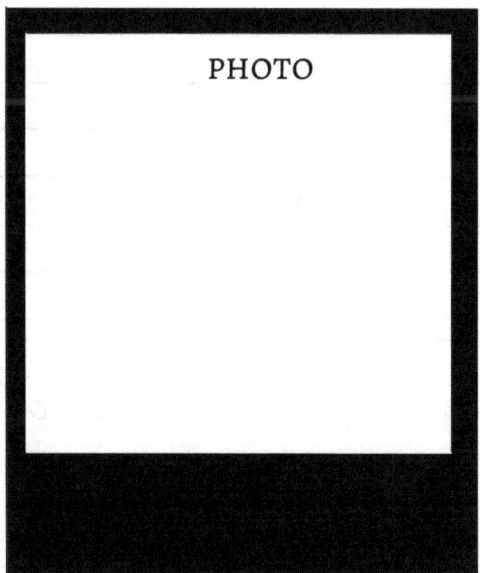

PHOTO

It's Our Anniversary!

ANNIVERSARY YEAR _____

CELEBRATING _____ YEARS

·················· *How we Celebrated* ··················

_____
_____
_____
_____
_____
_____
_____
_____
_____
_____

·················· *What Our Year Was Like* ··················

_____
_____
_____
_____
_____
_____
_____
_____
_____
_____

Highlights

Challenges

Plans & Goals for the Next Year

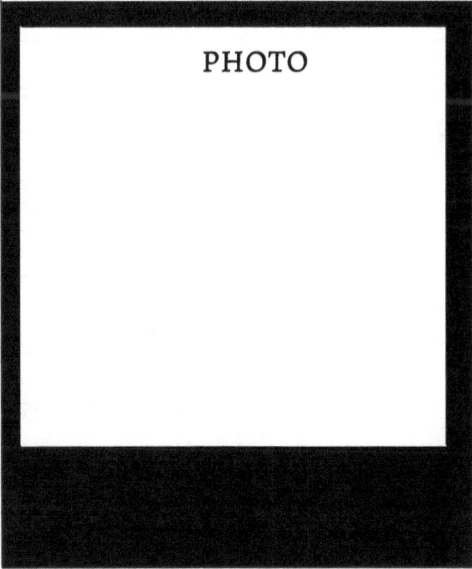

PHOTO

It's Our Anniversary!

ANNIVERSARY YEAR _____

CELEBRATING _____ YEARS

.... *How we Celebrated* ....

_____
_____
_____
_____
_____
_____
_____
_____
_____

.... *What Our Year Was Like* ....

_____
_____
_____
_____
_____
_____
_____
_____
_____

Highlights

Challenges

Plans & Goals for the Next Year

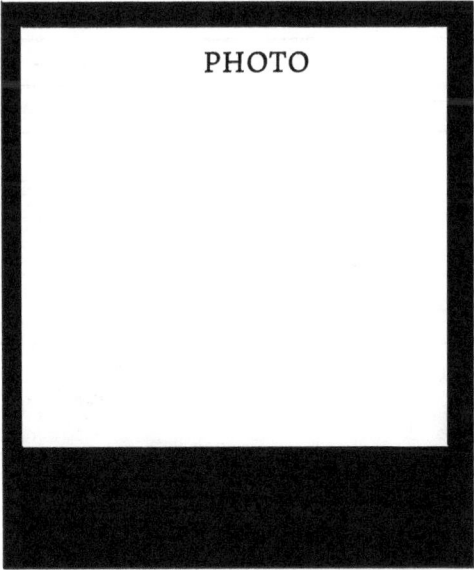

PHOTO

It's Our Anniversary!

ANNIVERSARY YEAR _____

CELEBRATING _____ YEARS

·················· *How we Celebrated* ··················

_____
_____
_____
_____
_____
_____
_____
_____
_____
_____

·················· *What Our Year Was Like* ··················

_____
_____
_____
_____
_____
_____
_____
_____

Highlights

Challenges

Plans & Goals for the Next Year

....

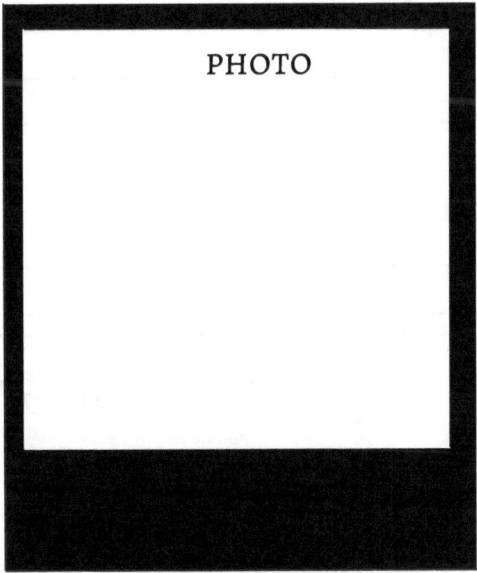

PHOTO

It's Our Anniversary!

ANNIVERSARY YEAR _____

CELEBRATING _____ YEARS

·················· *How we Celebrated* ··················

_____
_____
_____
_____
_____
_____
_____
_____
_____
_____

·················· *What Our Year Was Like* ··················

_____
_____
_____
_____
_____
_____
_____
_____
_____

Highlights

Challenges

Plans & Goals for the Next Year

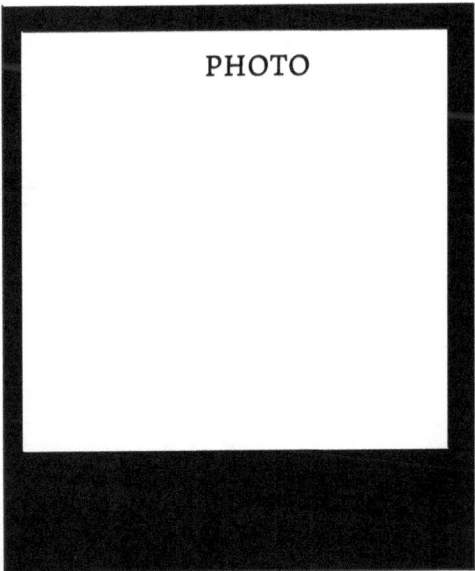

PHOTO

It's Our Anniversary!

ANNIVERSARY YEAR _____

CELEBRATING _____ YEARS

·················· *How we Celebrated* ··················

_____
_____
_____
_____
_____
_____
_____
_____
_____

·················· *What Our Year Was Like* ··················

_____
_____
_____
_____
_____
_____
_____
_____
_____

Highlights

Challenges

Plans & Goals for the Next Year

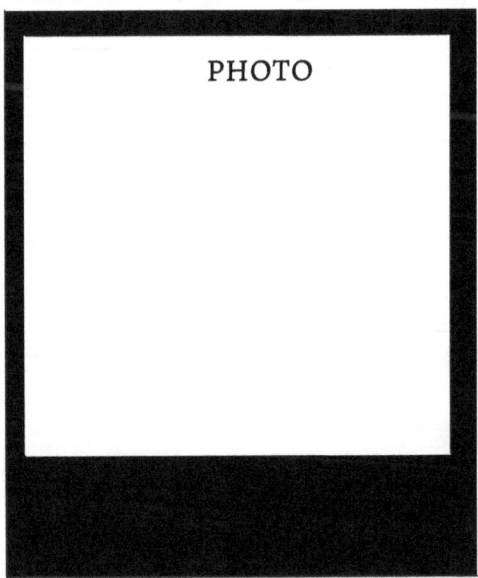

PHOTO

It's Our Anniversary!

ANNIVERSARY YEAR _____

CELEBRATING _____ YEARS

·················· How we Celebrated ··················

_____

_____

_____

_____

_____

_____

_____

_____

_____

·················· What Our Year Was Like ··················

_____

_____

_____

_____

_____

_____

_____

_____

_____

Highlights

Challenges

Plans & Goals for the Next Year

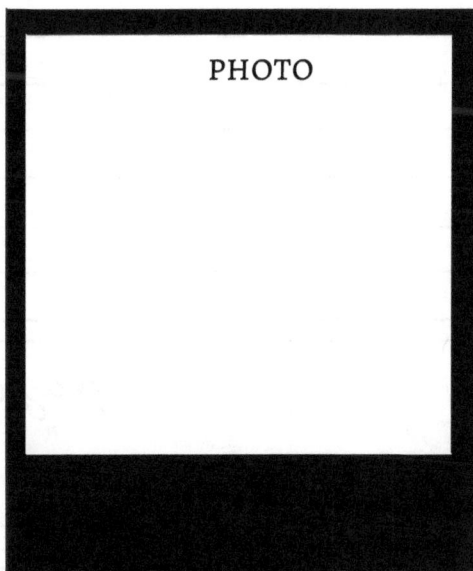

PHOTO

It's Our Anniversary!

ANNIVERSARY YEAR _____

CELEBRATING _____ YEARS

.... *How we Celebrated* ....

_____
_____
_____
_____
_____
_____
_____
_____
_____

.... *What Our Year Was Like* ....

_____
_____
_____
_____
_____
_____
_____
_____
_____
_____

Highlights

Challenges

Plans & Goals for the Next Year

⁃⁃⁃⁃⁃⁃⁃⁃⁃⁃⁃⁃⁃⁃⁃⁃⁃⁃⁃⁃⁃

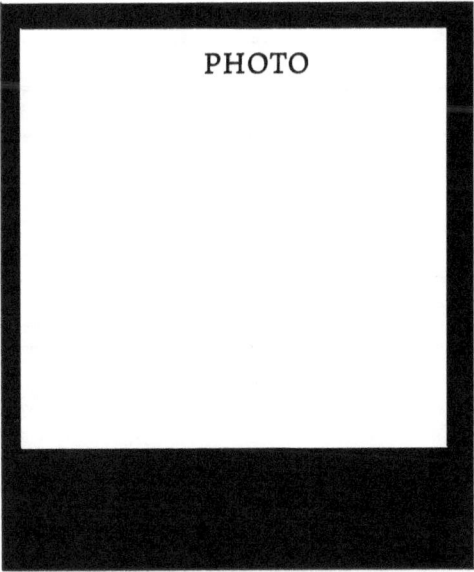

PHOTO

It's Our Anniversary!

ANNIVERSARY YEAR _____

CELEBRATING _____ YEARS

·················· How we Celebrated ··················

_____
_____
_____
_____
_____
_____
_____
_____
_____

·················· What Our Year Was Like ··················

_____
_____
_____
_____
_____
_____
_____
_____
_____

Highlights

Challenges

Plans & Goals for the Next Year

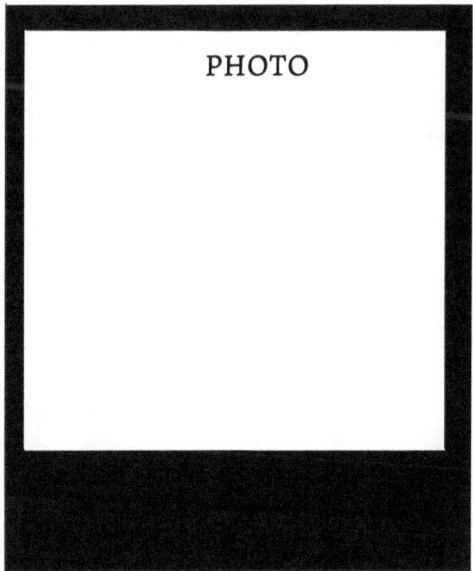

PHOTO

It's Our Anniversary!

ANNIVERSARY YEAR _____

CELEBRATING _____ YEARS

·················· *How we Celebrated* ··················

_____
_____
_____
_____
_____
_____
_____
_____
_____

·················· *What Our Year Was Like* ··················

_____
_____
_____
_____
_____
_____
_____
_____
_____

Highlights

Challenges

Plans & Goals for the Next Year

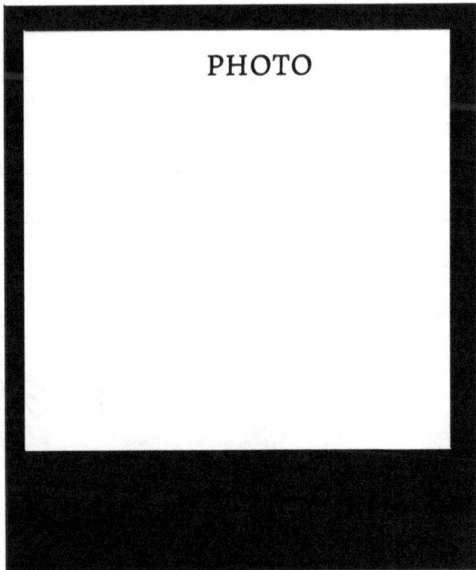

PHOTO

It's Our Anniversary!

ANNIVERSARY YEAR _____

CELEBRATING _____ YEARS

.... *How we Celebrated* ....

_____

_____

_____

_____

_____

_____

_____

_____

_____

.... *What Our Year Was Like* ....

_____

_____

_____

_____

_____

_____

_____

_____

_____

Highlights

Challenges

Plans & Goals for the Next Year

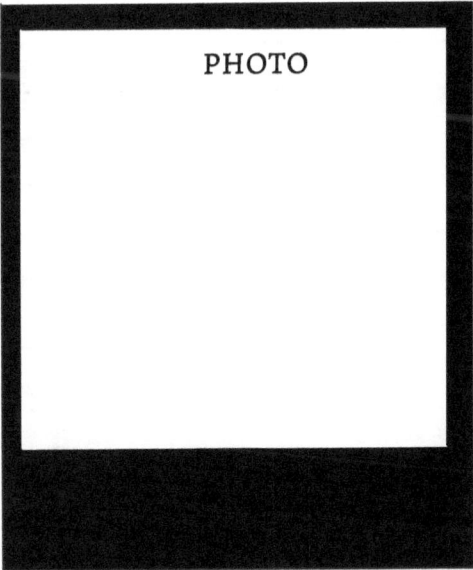

PHOTO

It's Our Anniversary!

ANNIVERSARY YEAR _____

CELEBRATING _____ YEARS

···················· How we Celebrated ····················

_____
_____
_____
_____
_____
_____
_____
_____
_____

···················· What Our Year Was Like ····················

_____
_____
_____
_____
_____
_____
_____
_____

Highlights

Challenges

Plans & Goals for the Next Year

_____
_____
_____
_____
_____
_____

• •

_____

_____

_____

_____

_____

_____

_____

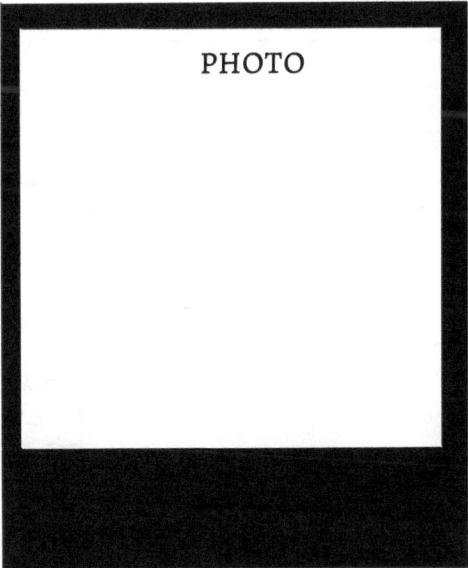

PHOTO

It's Our Anniversary!

ANNIVERSARY YEAR _____

CELEBRATING _____ YEARS

·················· *How we Celebrated* ··················

_____
_____
_____
_____
_____
_____
_____
_____
_____

·················· *What Our Year Was Like* ··················

_____
_____
_____
_____
_____
_____
_____
_____
_____

Highlights

Challenges

Plans & Goals for the Next Year

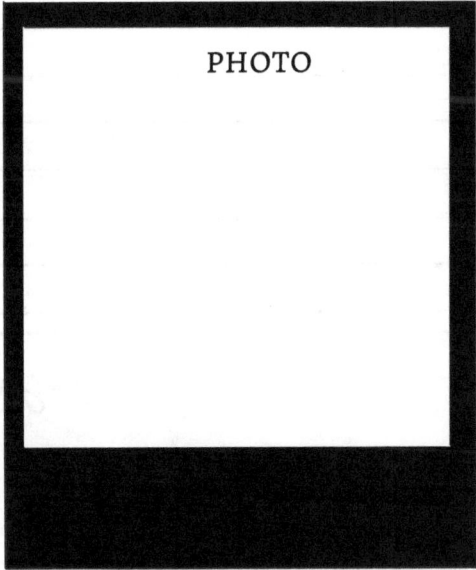

PHOTO

It's Our Anniversary!

ANNIVERSARY YEAR _____

CELEBRATING _____ YEARS

·················· How we Celebrated ··················

_____

_____

_____

_____

_____

_____

_____

_____

·················· What Our Year Was Like ··················

_____

_____

_____

_____

_____

_____

_____

_____

Highlights

Challenges

Plans & Goals for the Next Year

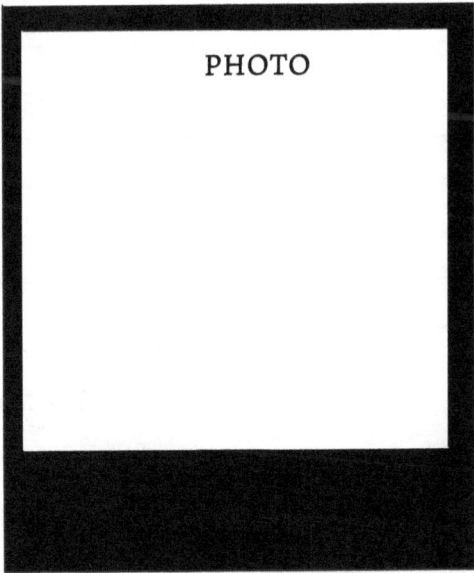

PHOTO

It's Our Anniversary!

ANNIVERSARY YEAR _____

CELEBRATING _____ YEARS

·················· How we Celebrated ··················

_____

_____

_____

_____

_____

_____

_____

_____

·················· What Our Year Was Like ··················

_____

_____

_____

_____

_____

_____

_____

_____

Highlights

Challenges

Plans & Goals for the Next Year

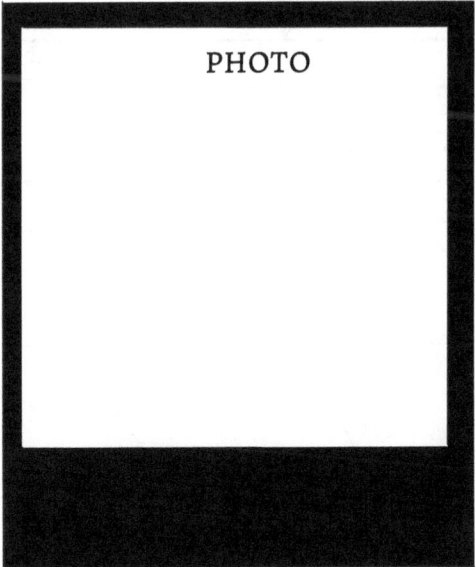

PHOTO

It's Our Anniversary!

ANNIVERSARY YEAR _____

CELEBRATING _____ YEARS

·················· *How we Celebrated* ··················

_____
_____
_____
_____
_____
_____
_____
_____
_____

·················· *What Our Year Was Like* ··················

_____
_____
_____
_____
_____
_____
_____
_____
_____

Highlights

Challenges

Plans & Goals for the Next Year

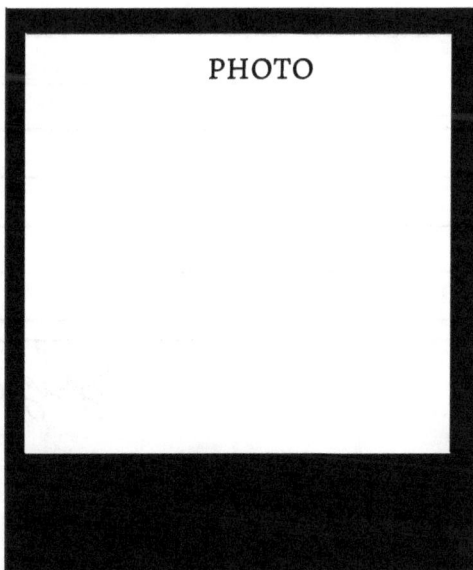

PHOTO

It's Our Anniversary!

ANNIVERSARY YEAR _____

CELEBRATING _____ YEARS

················· *How we Celebrated* ·················

_____

_____

_____

_____

_____

_____

_____

_____

_____

················· *What Our Year Was Like* ·················

_____

_____

_____

_____

_____

_____

_____

_____

Highlights

Challenges

Plans & Goals for the Next Year

....

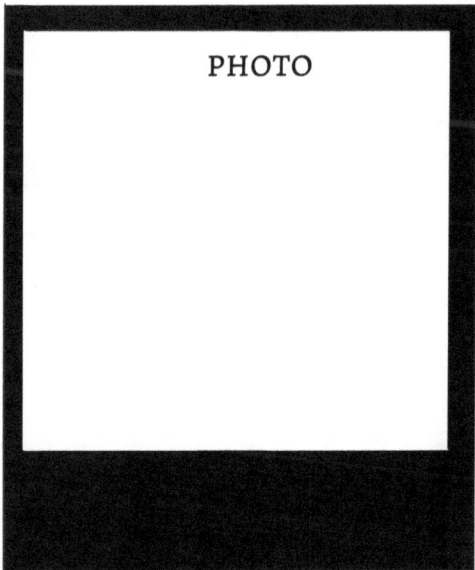

PHOTO

It's Our Anniversary!

ANNIVERSARY YEAR _____

CELEBRATING _____ YEARS

·················· *How we Celebrated* ··················

_____
_____
_____
_____
_____
_____
_____
_____
_____
_____

··············· *What Our Year Was Like* ···············

_____
_____
_____
_____
_____
_____
_____
_____
_____
_____

Highlights

Challenges

Plans & Goals for the Next Year

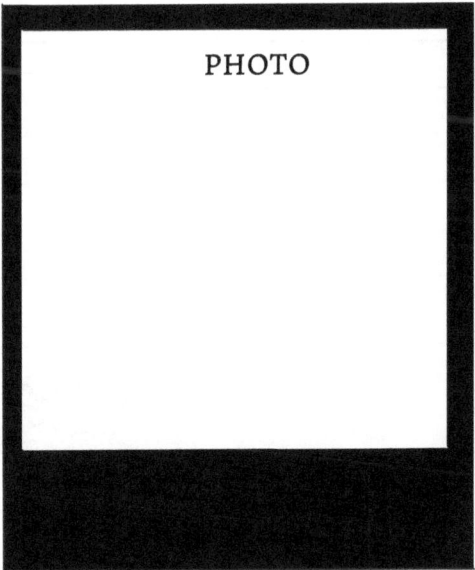

PHOTO

It's Our Anniversary!

ANNIVERSARY YEAR _____

CELEBRATING _____ YEARS

·············· *How we Celebrated* ··············

_____
_____
_____
_____
_____
_____
_____
_____
_____
_____
_____
_____

·············· *What Our Year Was Like* ··············

_____
_____
_____
_____
_____
_____
_____
_____
_____
_____
_____
_____

Highlights

Challenges

Plans & Goals for the Next Year

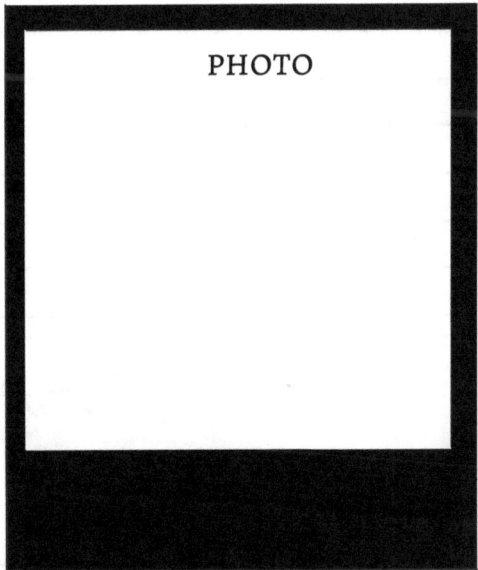

_____

_____

_____

_____

_____

_____

. . . .

_____

_____

_____

_____

_____

_____

_____

PHOTO

It's Our Anniversary!

ANNIVERSARY YEAR _____

CELEBRATING _____ YEARS

·········· *How we Celebrated* ··········

_____

_____

_____

_____

_____

_____

_____

_____

_____

·········· *What Our Year Was Like* ··········

_____

_____

_____

_____

_____

_____

_____

_____

_____

Highlights

Challenges

Plans & Goals for the Next Year

_____
_____
_____
_____
_____
_____
_____

• •

_____

_____

_____

_____

_____

_____

_____

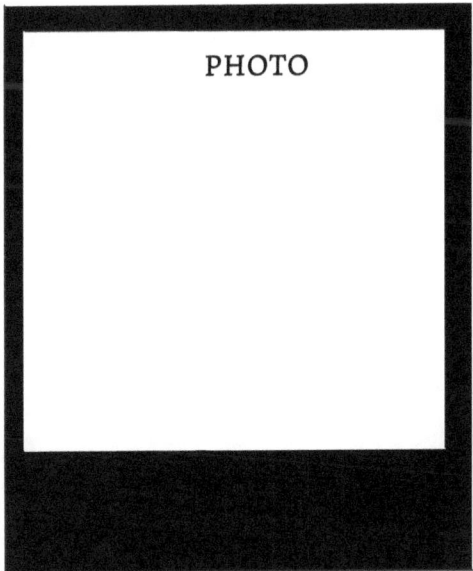

PHOTO

www.ingramcontent.com/pod-product-compliance
Lightning Source LLC
Chambersburg PA
CBHW051034030426
42336CB00015B/2865